Published in the USA by Candle Books
ISBN 0 8254 7260 1
Distributed by Kregel Publications, PO Box 2607
Grand Rapids, Michigan 49501

Illustrations by Martin Pierce
Text by Tim Dowley

Worldwide co-edition organized and produced by
Angus Hudson Ltd,
Concorde House
Grenville Place, Mill Hill,
London NW7 3SA, England
Tel: +44 20 8959 3668
Fax: +44 20 8959 3678

Printed in Italy

CANDLE BOOKS
GRAND RAPIDS, MICHIGAN

How to use this book

- Each picture has some missing parts. Read the question and then rub the invisible areas with the edge of a coin to find the hidden drawings.
- Read the story of Moses in the book.
- Look up the story of Moses in the Bible verses listed on each page.
- Color the completed pictures with felt-tip pens or colored pencils.
- Each picture has a hidden snake. Search carefully to find them all—they're in "invisible" ink too!

Pharaoh of Egypt ordered every Jewish baby boy to be killed. To save her baby, Moses' mother put him in a basket. Rub the invisible part of the picture with the edge of a coin to see what is floating in the water.

Look up the story of Moses in the bulrushes in Exodus 2:1–4.

Have you found the snake in this picture?

Soon the princess of Egypt came to the river to bathe. She saw the baby. "He's beautiful," she said. "Bring him to the palace to live." Rub the invisible part of the picture with the edge of a coin to see who found baby Moses.

Look up the story of Moses and the princess in Exodus 2:5–7.

Have you found the snake in this picture?

So Moses grew up in Pharaoh's palace. The princess of Egypt brought him up like a prince.
Rub the invisible part of the picture with the edge of a coin to see what the servants are doing.
Look up the story of Moses in the palace in Exodus 2:8–10.
Have you found the snake in this picture?

The Jewish people were slaves in Egypt. Moses watched as they were forced to drag huge stones to build the pyramids.
Rub the invisible part of the picture with the edge of a coin to see who is pulling the stone.

Look up the story of Moses and his people in Exodus 2:11.

Have you found the snake in this picture?

Moses didn't forget that he was Jewish. One day he say an Egyptian soldier beating a Jewish slave. He was very angry and killed the soldier. Rub the invisible part of the picture with the edge of a coin to see if anyone was watching.

Look up the story of Moses and the cruel Egyptian in Exodus 2:11–14.

Have you found the snake in this picture?

Moses knew it wouldn't be long before he was found out. So he ran away from the palace.
Rub the invisible part of the picture with the edge of a coin to see if anyone has noticed Moses.
Look up the story of Moses' escape from Egypt in Exodus 2:15.
Have you found the snake in this picture?

Moses didn't stop running away until he reached the desert. There he looked after sheep. It was a very different way of life.
Rub the invisible part of the picture with the edge of a coin to find what is in the desert.
Look up the story of Moses in the desert in Exodus 2:15–25.

Have you found the snake in this picture?

One day in the desert Moses was amazed to see a bush on fire but not burning up. God said "I am sending you to rescue your people from Egypt." Rub the invisible part of the picture with the edge of a coin to find what Moses saw.

Look up the story of Moses and the burning bush in Exodus 3:1–21.

Have you found the snake in this picture?

Moses went with his brother, Aaron, to tell Pharaoh, "Let our people go!" Aaron turned his rod into a snake to show God was powerful. But the magicians did the same! Rub the invisible part of the picture with the edge of a coin to see what's on the floor.

Look up the story of Moses and Aaron in Exodus 7:8–13.

Have you found the snake in this picture?

Moses went to Pharaoh again, saying, "Let my people go." But Pharaoh refused. God sent a horde of frogs throughout Egypt.
Rub the invisible part of the picture with the edge of a coin to see why the cook is scared.
Look up the story of the horde of frogs in Exodus 8:1–15.
Have you found the snake in this picture?

Moses went to Pharaoh again, saying, "Let my people go." But Pharaoh refused. God sent hail and thunder throughout Egypt. Rub the invisible part of the picture with the edge of a coin to see why the people are running to get indoors.

Look up the story of the hail storms in Exodus 9:13–35.

Have you found the snake in this picture?

Moses went to Pharaoh yet again, saying, "Let my people go." At last Pharaoh said, "Go—and take your people with you." Rub the invisible part of the picture with the edge of a coin to learn who Moses is talking to.

Look up the story of Moses' meeting with Pharaoh in Exodus 10:21–29.

Have you found the snake in this picture?

Before they left, each family painted lamb's blood over their door. That night every Egyptian oldest son died, but the houses marked by blood were safe. Rub the invisible part of the picture to see what the people are looking at.

Look up the story of the Passover in Exodus 12:1–13.

Have you found the snake in this picture?

Grabbing everything they could carry—food, clothing, pots and pans—the Jewish people left Egypt to walk to the land God promised them. Rub the invisible part of the picture with the edge of a coin to see if many Israelites are leaving Egypt.

Look up the story of the escape from Egypt in Exodus 12:21–42.

Have you found the snake in this picture?

Soon they came to the Red Sea—but the Egyptians were chasing them! Moses held out his hand, the water parted, and the Israelites walked safely across. Rub the invisible part of the picture with the edge of a coin to see who is trapped in the water.

Look up the story of crossing the Red Sea in Exodus 14.

Have you found the snake in this picture?

Soon the people were grumbling, "There's not enough food here. Let's go back to Egypt!" So God sent special food called manna for them to collect and eat. Rub the invisible part of the picture with the edge of a coin to see what the children are doing.

Look up the story of the manna in Exodus 16.

Have you found the snake in this picture?

Next the people grew thirsty! "We shall die in this hot desert," they moaned. So God told Moses to strike a rock with his stick—and water gushed out. Rub the invisible part of the picture with the edge of a coin to see what Moses is hitting.

Look up the story of water from the rock in Exodus 17:1–6.

Have you found the snake in this picture?

When Moses came down Mount Sinai with the Ten Commandments on stone tablets, he was very angry. The people had turned away from God and were worshipping something else. Rub the invisible part of the picture with the edge of a coin to see what they were worshipping.

Look up the story of the Ten Commandments in Exodus 20 and 32

Have you found the snake in this picture?

The people told God they were sorry for making an idol out of gold. Moses went up the mountain again and came back with new stone tablets. Rub the invisible part of the picture with the edge of a coin to see who the Israelites are greeting.

Look up the story of Moses and the new stone tablets in Exodus 34.

Have you found the snake in this picture?

In the desert Moses and the people built a special tent where they could meet God. It was beautifully decorated with cloth, silver, and gold. Rub the invisible part of the picture with the edge of a coin to see what the carpenter is doing.

Look up the story of the special tent in Exodus 36:8–38.

Have you found the snake in this picture?

When the tent was finished, the priests carried the ark of God inside. It was put in a room called "The Holiest Place." Rub the invisible part of the picture with the edge of a coin to see what the priests are carrying.

Look up the story of the ark of God in Exodus 25:10–22.

Have you found the snake in this picture?

When Moses was old, he looked toward the Promised Land, but he knew he would never live there. He had brought his people to the end of their desert journey. Rub the invisible part of the picture with the edge of a coin to see what Moses is looking at.

Look up the story of the death of Moses in Deuteronomy 34.

Have you found the snake in this picture?